HOW TO MAKE YOUR CREDIT SCORE SOAR

By Julie Marie McDonough

FriesenPress

Suite 300 - 990 Fort St

Victoria, BC, Canada, V8V 3K2

www.friesenpress.com

Copyright © 2015 by Julie Marie McDonough

First Edition — 2015

All rights reserved.

No part of this publication may be reproduced in any form, or by any means, electronic or mechanical, including photocopying, recording, or any information browsing, storage, or retrieval system, without permission in writing from the publisher.

ISBN

978-1-4602-5775-3 (Hardcover)

978-1-4602-5776-0 (Paperback)

978-1-4602-5777-7 (eBook)

1. Business & Economics, Personal Finance, Money Management

Distributed to the trade by The Ingram Book Company

CONTENTS

Acknowledgements	v
Introduction	vii
About The Author	ix
Chapter 1:	
Credit Score Principles	1
What Is A Credit Score	3
What Is FICO And What Do The Numbers Mean	7
What Makes Up My Credit Score	11
I Can Raise My Credit Score By Myself	15
The "Big Three" Reporting Bureaus	19
How You Can Avoid Credit Report Mistakes	23
How Do Inquiries Effect My Credit	25
Chapter 2:	
Your Free Credit Report And Planning Ahead	27
How To Get Your Free Credit Report	29
How To Read Your Credit Report	31
How To Dispute And To Whom	35
How To Spot Identity Theft	39
How Long Will Negative Marks Stay On My Report	45
Stategic Planning To Maintain An Already Good Score	49
Is Monitoring For Me	53
Chapter 3:	
Increasing Your Credit Score Made Easy	57
Simple Steps To Improve Your Credit Score	59
How To Negotiate Debt	69
How Many Lines Of Credit Should I Have	73

On-Line Bill Paying	77
Credit Myths	79
Be Diligent and Don't Give Up	81

Chapter 4:
Building Credit and Budgeting   85

Living Within Your Means And Learning To Budget	87
New Credit Users And Building Credit	93
Good Credit Habits	97
Your Credit And Real Estate Loan Requests	99
Tri-Merged Reports	103
Teaching Teens About Credit	105
How Your Credit Can Impact Your Job Search	109
Let's "Soar." Life Is Better With Good Credit	113
Credit Terminology And Acronyms	115
Consumer Resources	119
Disclaimer:	121

ACKNOWLEDGEMENTS

I would like to thank my family for their continued encouragement and support. Special thanks to my sister, PJ, who was there to help me with many aspects of the book including the title. My appreciation to my two amazing children, Amanda and Andrew, who always make me proud and my husband, who is my rock, for understanding me and accepting me for the workaholic that I am.

I would like to dedicate this book to my mother. I grew up in a family of six children with one income that never reached quite far enough. My parents always struggled financially, but hid it well. My siblings and I never lacked anything we really needed in life, but we didn't have extravagant things either. The need-and-want list in our household was always limited to a need list. I learned a lot from growing up without a silver spoon in my mouth.

Thanks to my previous clients, for without you, I would not have written this book in an effort to help others.

As I turn another page in my own chapter of life, I have come to realize how important it is to cherish those around you, share your knowledge and help those that are in need.

INTRODUCTION

Increasing and maintaining your credit scores is serious business. Your credit score is a crucial enabler in today's way of life. There is something to be said for a person who knows how to manipulate their credit score. Your credit score can determine whether, or not, you can obtain financial services and the cost of a car loan, mortgage, insurance, and credit cards. You're credit score can even weigh-in on whether or not you get that job you applied for. Fair? Maybe not, but it is the new reality.

I will address a lot of detailed information in order to provide you with all the tools you need to increase your credit score. It doesn't matter what your score is today, because we are going to improve it.

After reading this book and applying the information, your score should increase substantially. Yes, this may take a little time, but isn't your credit worthiness worth it? Yes, of course it is. This book can help everyone. It doesn't matter if you are currently behind on payments, filed bankruptcy, currently in default on your mortgage or you are struggling from paycheck to paycheck. It will also help those of you who have sold a home in a short-sale, went through a loan modification and even those who have good credit and want GREAT credit.

Regardless of where your credit is today, I will help you understand that you are the sole owner of your credit destiny. I have dedicated over twenty-five years helping consumers, like you, clean their credit, become homeowners and put their financial house in order. Learn how a credit score is created, how to recover from bad credit, how to remove errors on your credit report and how to maximize your personal credit score. There are some amazing secrets I'm going to teach you that will help to make your Credit Score SOAR.

ABOUT THE AUTHOR

Julie Marie McDonough has more than twenty-eight years' experience as a real estate broker, loan broker, and credit consultant. She started her career in the mortgage lending industry in 1985 and quickly learned the importance of customer service and self-motivation. After spending some time in management, she and her husband, Joseph, formed their own mortgage company in 1988. A few years later they added real estate services to the company's offerings, and still later, Julie added credit-consulting services. Today, AmeriSell Advantage Properties, AmeriSell Mortgage, and AmeriSell Credit Consulting offer homebuyers all the services they need, under one roof.

Julie is a consumer advocate and speaker who has helped countless people correct errors on their credit reports so they can optimize their credit scores and get the best mortgage rates possible when purchasing a home. Some of her credit-consulting clients refer to her as a miracle worker. Julie is recognized for her vast knowledge in the industry and is sought out for her expertise.

Julie and her husband live near Los Angeles with their two children. She is a member of the National Association of Credit Services Organization (NACSO), National Association of Realtors (NAR), California Association of Realtors (CAR), National Notary Association (NNA), National Association of Professional Women (NAPW) and the United States Tennis Association (USTA). Julie enjoys playing league tennis and traveling.

CHAPTER 1:

Credit Score Principles

What Is A Credit Score

A credit score is a number assessment given to rate your performance as it relates to the following:

- your payment history
- balance owed on accounts
- length of time you have established accounts
- new accounts
- the type(s) of credit you have

These are the five most important criteria you should know about your credit regarding how your credit is assessed and viewed. That may sound a bit simple, but that is far from the truth. We are going to focus on the five techniques you can use to increase your credit score and avoid the, greater than, eighty-eight ways to decrease it. By tending to these five key success factors, you can maximize your potential score in the shortest period of time. Our goal is to make this objective easier for you to obtain than if you tried to discover all these factors by yourself. I will provide you with valuable information so you can expedite the process.

A credit score is identified as a three digit number that takes into account the information provided by all your creditors. Each creditor reports your credit payment history to one or more credit bureaus. There are a total of three major credit bureaus or agencies. You create the data that forms your own scores as you manage your financial affairs. Let me provide a clarification. A creditor is an institution to whom you owe money, like a mortgage company or a credit card company that grants you credit. You may think of it as one of the companies you make your payments to each month. A credit bureau is a separate entity that receives your creditor's payment reports, typically for each month's payment. Every time you make a payment, open a new line of credit or use a credit card, the creditor reports that information to the credit bureaus and your credit report, along with your credit score, is compiled.

Each time a creditor reports to the credit bureaus, there is a potential risk for adverse information. Your scores are constantly changing, and information reported to, one or more, of the credit bureaus is updated throughout the month. You will receive one credit score from each of the three independent credit bureaus, providing you have enough data to rate a score. In total, you will have three different scores. Everything you financially do matters to your credit.

Your three digit credit score will define you as a credit worthy consumer. Those three little numbers, side-by-side in a sequence that sometimes we wish could be changed, may determine how you live the rest of your life. It can determine how much you pay for products and services and whether or not you will be approved or denied for things you want and need. Yes, we are all affected by this three-digit numeric. These three numbers will continually change, whether we want them to or not. Some trade lines on your credit report can change this number much more than others. Every day of every week of every month, whether it is from an action or from just the simple passage of time, each consumer's credit report is changing. You can say that credit reports have a life of their own. Because your credit score is constantly changing, you have to stay focused and monitor your credit. I'm not saying that you have to pay for an outside credit monitoring company; however, I am a firm believer that you should know what is going on with your own credit. I'll show you how to do that later in the book.

What Is FICO And What Do The Numbers Mean

FICO is an acronym for Fair Isaac Credit Company. FICO scores range from 300-850. "Why is this?" you may ask. It is because the Fair Isaac initial model ran from 100-299. So when they decided to scratch that model, they scratched the numeric also. The FICO Score was named after the inventors of the credit risk score. FICO is a three-digit number that quantifies your credit risk, which is your ability to pay debts and your payment history. There are many credit-scoring models in existence, but the one that is most widely used is the FICO credit score. Approximately ninety percent of all financial institutions in the United States use FICO scores in their decision-making. It is essential that your credit report be correct and complete, because your credit score is extremely important. Your credit score is determined by a mathematical algorithm using information from your existing creditors and the data they report to the credit bureaus. It intends to predict risk. Specifically, it quantifies the probability that you will become seriously delinquent on your credit obligations in the two years after the scoring takes place.

What does the FICO number mean? The higher the number is, the better the score and the higher the probability that you will pay your obligations on time. A higher number

Julie Marie McDonough

indicates a lower credit risk to financial institutions and creditors. Your goal is to achieve the highest number possible in order to maximize your financial options. It almost sounds like a game with the basic rule being; make your payments on time every month to accomplish positive steps forward. Pay obligations late, or go into default, and you take ten steps back. Okay, so this game can be pretty harsh if you falter. However, I assure you that the benefits of paying your debt on time and moving forward, is well worth the effort.

Personal or demographic information such as age, race, address, marital status, income and employment, do not affect the score. FICO does not distinguish between consumers that make $24,000 or $240,000 a year. It doesn't take under consideration how old you are or how many dependents you might have. Let me explain further. Let's take a nineteen year old college student, who is working part-time and making just enough to put himself through community college while living at home with his parents, and compare this person to a forty-two year old man, who has a college degree from USC, is working full time in Electrical Engineering making six figures, owns his own home, and is married with two children in private school. Both have totally different lifestyles and obligations. They don't have much in common at all, except their credit scores. Both have a 725 FICO middle score.

Why, you may ask? Why doesn't the man, who has already graduated from college and has a great paying job, have a better score than the student living on the edge with his parents? FICO doesn't acknowledge that detail of information. FICO only takes under consideration the risk model involved in granting credit. How likely is it that the consumer, if offered a line of credit or loan, will repay the loan? Credit scores determine this based on algorithms, a mathematical method, used to quantify the risk for the lender. Remember, the scores are not taking age, race, address, marital status, income or employment under consideration at all. You can be ninety-nine years old, married to a twenty-two year old, who has one million dollars in a trust fund, neither with a job, living in a remote area without cell service or internet, and it would have no bearing on your credit score.

FICO 9 is coming and will change the current model. It is intended to give lenders the transparency they need to make better lending decisions at the same time helping consumers by giving more specificity to the score impacting credit report items. Here are some of the highlights:

Collections: Medical events are unfortunate and often unavoidable. This type of debt is not standard or voluntary, therefore it was improperly coded. The new model will now put less score weight on unpaid medical collections and some collections will have no weight at all. This will allow consumers to address the issues without long-term effects left on their credit. However, other collections, such as a defaulted credit card, unpaid cell phone bill or utility bill, will have similar weight as they did in previous scoring models.

Rental Payments: Just because tenants do not own the home they live in, doesn't negate the fact that it is the largest payment they may make in their lifetime. With the FICO 9 model, rental payments can be factored into the consumer's credit score as long as it is reported and tracked through an approved service like https://www.renttrack.com. This will not only give consumers the ability to build a stronger profile, it gives property owners and landlords a higher likelihood that their rents will be paid on time by incorporating this element into the credit report and FICO score.

WHAT MAKES UP MY CREDIT SCORE

Data from your credit report goes into five major categories that make up the scoring model and weighs some factors more heavily, such as payment history and amounts owed.

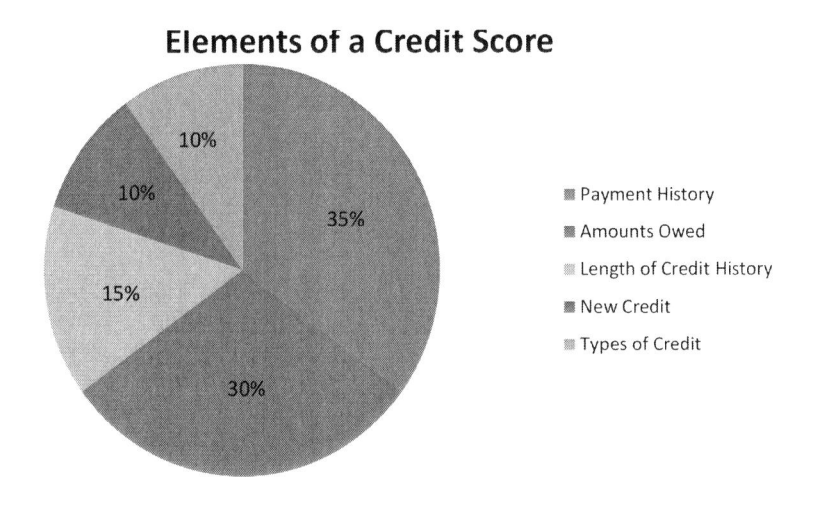

Elements of a Credit Score

- 35% Payment History
- 30% Amounts Owed
- 15% Length of Credit History
- 10% New Credit
- 10% Types of Credit

THE FIVE ELEMENTS OF ELEVATION

Payment history: (35 percent) -Your account payment information. Have you paid your creditors on time or late? This will include any delinquencies and public records.

Amounts owed: (30 percent) – Also referred to as credit utilization. How much you owe on your accounts? The amount of available credit you're using on revolving accounts is heavily weighted. What percentage of the credit limit are you using? Credit scores are negatively affected when you are at or near your credit limit.

Length of credit history: (15 percent) - How long ago you opened accounts and the time since account activity.

New credit: (10 percent) - Your pursuit of new credit, including credit inquiries and the number of recently opened accounts.

Types of credit used: (10 percent) - The mix of accounts you have, such as revolving (i.e.: credit cards) and installment (i.e.: mortgage, auto loans).

I refer to these as the "Five Elements of Elevation." Every time you make a payment, every line of credit you open, and the amount you owe verses your credit limit all matter. Each of these five categories affects a formula impacting success. How much you spend and how often you pay your bills will affect your credit score. If you pay your bills on time, you will receive better interest rates and have easier access to credit. Pay your bills late, and you will lower your FICO score which will also result in more costly financing and fewer financial options. In addition, if you have a credit card with an introductory rate, one late payment can increase the rate dramatically for any balances you may carry.

"Why am I being rated?" "Can I opt out?" The easy answer is yes, you can. However, opting-out means you pay cash for everything; cars, houses, boats, food, entertainment, large appliances, everything. Even if you pay cash, from here forward, if you have already used credit then the use of credit may have already determined your credit score, whether you wanted it to or not.

Many people choose to live a life style above and beyond what they can actually afford. Doing so means they live on credit. They choose to put the minimum down on large purchases like a house or car. Due to the availability of credit, people buy things they don't need and pay too much for the things they do. Credit card companies have made it easy to lure you in and actually entice you. They offer promotions like free airplane miles, hats, beach bags, shopping dollars, and yes, even cash back. You apply for their credit card and they will give you cash back on all your purchases. It's so easy.

But wait, is paying, perhaps up to 25% interest for many years, on your groceries, clothes, gas, etc...worth it? I say, let them keep the flyer miles you never use, the hat you don't wear, the canvas beach bag that is still in plastic in your closet, and yes, even the 1% cash back. If you cannot pay the balance in-full at the end of each billing cycle, PAY CASH! Why? Think about it, they are giving you 1% cash back for purchasing a product that you want and you pay them up to 25% interest. Who is kidding who? They are winning at this game. Are we all just so excited for instant gratification, and to get something for nothing, that we forgot to check and see how much "nothing" is costing us? Wake up people! Always be aware of the terms under which you are borrowing money. Put on the glasses, get out the magnify glass and read the details. Nothing in life is truly free, someone is paying for it and that someone is usually you. When you think something is too good to be true, it usually is. Now, I know this may sound like the "glass is half empty" story, but I used to be an optimist and now I find myself as more of a realist after seeing hundreds of individual financial situations over the decades. I am realistic about the effects of credit and what it can do for and against people. Beware the fine print my friends.

I Can Raise My Credit Score By Myself

Yes, you can increase your score without any help from anyone else. You do not have to pay thousands of dollars to a "credit fix-it-up company" for what you could and should be doing yourself. No one else will take as much interest in your financial affairs as yourself. You should be using the money you would pay others to pay your own bills. There are too many "credit fix-it-up companies" that claim they can remove all delinquent or negative items off your credit report. Do you truly believe that they can remove bankruptcies, judgments, late payments and liens? No one can legally make that claim. I hear horror stories from people who have gone through scams like these. They paid thousands to credit-fix-it companies with no or disappointing results. It is heart retching to hear the aftermath. Do not rely on scam artists. Fix your credit yourself, save thousands, and be sure it is done accurately and timely.

I will show you how to get your own credit report for FREE. I will then teach you how to read the report and identify incorrect or misinformation that could be damaging your credit score. I will explain how to dispute accounts. If you follow all the instructions I will provide, you can do it yourself and your credit score will increase. There are a lot of very busy people who do not have time for the dispute process. There are also lazy people, who would rather pay someone else to review their credit and go through the process for them.

For those of you who choose to use an outside credit-fixing company, check them out thoroughly to make sure that the company is reputable? The Better Business Bureau (BBB) is a good reference. Did you know that it is illegal for a credit repair agency to take money up-front from you? I find that currently the most popular process is a pay per deletion. You only pay after they accomplish the deletion of the debt. Do not get caught-up in the pipe dream of thinking a company can remove a bankruptcy that you filed and is discharged. This is not likely. However, if the bankruptcy dates are incorrect or they did not report correct information (like a variance in a person's name), then you can dispute it. If the dispute is validated, then the credit bureaus will have to remove the misreporting. It is possible for a debt or creditor to remove an item, correct the disputed data and re-report. Disputing and documenting is something everyone can do for themselves. You do not have to pay good money to an outside company if you can do it yourself. Put the money toward paying off bills.

You may ask, "How much does each change I make affect my credit score"? The answer is usually "it depends," and for good reason. Credit score developers don't reveal the exact point increases or deductions. The weight of any given activity can also vary for different credit histories. Within a scoring model, there is more than one formula used to calculate a score, and each formula is designed for a category of consumers with similar credit profiles. The information in your credit report determines which formula is used. If you are a new credit user, for instance, the scoring model will put you into a category for people with young credit histories, and use a scoring formula specific to that group. We refer to each group as a score card.

In order to increase your credit score(s), you must understand what a credit score is made-up of and whether or not your credit report is reflecting true and accurate information. You have the right to dispute anything you feel is not correct.

THE "BIG THREE" REPORTING BUREAUS

There are three major credit reporting bureaus, Experian, Trans Union, and Equifax. They are referred to as the "Big Three." These reporting bureaus do not grant credit. They gather the information from your creditors and, using their independent credit models, provide data to others who want to know if you are (or are not) a good credit risk. As a process to do this effectively, they created their independent scoring models, like FICO. To make things a little more complex, you have more than one credit score. Each of the credit Bureaus has a separate score which usually differs. Sometimes it is a very slight difference, but I have seen where they have varied up to one hundred points. This is not common, but it can happen. The most common reason that they would differ is due to the creditors and who they report to. Let us say that your VISA credit card reports to Equifax and Trans Union, but not to Experian. This would be a perfect example on why scores are different. There are no mandatory rules that say every creditor must report their data to each of the "Big Three" bureaus. Experian, Trans Union, and Equifax are not the only players in town. Did you know that there are over 35 "other" credit bureaus? Here is a glimpse at some of them;

- Medical Information Bureau (MIB) – The MIB keeps tabs on your medical history.
- LexisNexis – collects public records from the PACER system and court houses.
- Chex Systems and Telecheck – are used for NSF and check fraud screening.
- Core Logic Teletrack and DataX – are used for Payday Lending Reporting
- Tenant Data Services and Leasing Desk – are used for Rental Screening
- Accurate Background, The Work Number and HireRight – are used for Employment
- National Consumer Telecom and Utilities Exchange – used for Utility Reporting

There are so many, and all of them collect data on you and have a specialized reason for doing so. They exist because there are businesses, creditors, landlords, banks and employers who want to know all about you and your habits. Remember, someone granting you credit or employing you wants to know if you are a good risk. The reporting bureaus shown above let creditors know if your mortgage or rent has been late, if you bounce checks, had a foreclosure, filed bankruptcy, have tax liens, pay your utility bills, have had an eviction and more. It's all available for a fee.

Many people think that Experian, Trans Union and Equifax, the "Big Three," are government run and operated agencies. This is incorrect. They are each separate, private, for profit companies. There is big money in gathering and selling data. This makes these three companies huge. They are regulated by the government and have to follow very specific, mandated guidelines. They are not government agencies.

(IMAGE COURTESY OF STUART MILES AT FREEDIGITALPHOTOS.NET)

How You Can Avoid Credit Report Mistakes

There are some very simple ways to avoid credit report mistakes. Take the time to complete forms thoroughly and completely. The information you provide is usually the information the creditor will be using to run your credit report. Double check and make sure your full name and social security number are correct. Be diligent in checking for misspellings in street names and cities of current and previous addresses.

Always put your full legal name on all documents. Too often a credit report is run as Jim or Jimmy instead of James. This causes future headaches. Do not do it. You should use the name as it appears on your birth certificate or driver's license. If you are applying for a home loan and your credit report does not match your identification, it creates extra work and sometimes denial on your loan application. If there are variances of your name on the report, you will be asked to provide or sign an "AKA" letter. AKA stands for Also Known As. If you are purchasing a home, you will have to have some documents notarized. You must have your name on the document(s) exactly as it appears on your identification. Any changes here and the notary will not be able to acknowledge the document. This can create tremendous challenges.

How Do Inquiries Effect My Credit

A standard credit application can cause a credit inquiry. This includes, but is not limited to, home loans, auto loans, personal loans or rental applications. These forms of applications create what is considered a hard inquiry. You are completing data or an application in an effort to acquire credit or housing and have the right to shop for goods and services. These inquiries will create a hard inquiry. In regards to a soft inquiry, your credit is checked, but it is not usually the result of an application. It is considered a soft inquiry when you run your own credit, access your monitoring service, or when a bank checks your credit to check to see if you would be a good candidate for a promotional credit card.

Hard inquires can negatively affect your FICO score. Hard inquiries are notification to the financial world that you are shopping and are going to make a purchase. Hard inquires can become a problem when you make numerous inquiries in a short period of time while shopping for a home loan, auto loan, personal loan, or credit cards. Be careful, they know you are shopping. A single inquiry can reduce your credit score anywhere between one to five points. If you complete an application for a new gas card in November so you can use it to travel to grandma's house for Thanksgiving and then fill out an application for a new credit card in December to buy Christmas gifts, you will have two separate hard inquiries on your credit report and each of them can affect your score up to five points each. That can be a hit of ten points. When you are looking to establish a new credit, it is a good idea to shop for the best deal. A hard inquiry is going to hit your score negatively, but if you bundle all similar inquiries over a two-week time frame, the inquiries will be seen as one, therefore impacting your credit score one time only. Some credit scoring models even allow a period up to forty-five days.

Your existing credit score will often determine if, and how many points, a hard inquiry will deduct from your score. For consumers with a credit history of making payments on time, with a low utilization rate, and a consistency of higher FICO scores, they may find little or no change on their score. For the not so careful credit user with maxed-out cards and a lot of delinquencies, a hard inquiry will have a greater negative impact on your credit score.

Soft inquiries are not something with which you should be overly concerned. They do not affect your score like the hard inquiries. There is no negative scoring associated with checking your own credit report once a year on https://www.annualcreditreport.com or through credit monitoring. Feel confident to maintain checking for changes or errors to your personal credit report with no negative impact.

CHAPTER 2:

Your Free Credit Report And Planning Ahead

How To Get Your Free Credit Report

Consumers have the right to a free credit report annually as mandated by Federal Law. You can receive one credit report from each credit reporting agency per year. The Federal Trade Commission (FTC) and Consumer Federal Protection Bureau (CFPB) acknowledge only one true free credit report source: https://www.annualcreditreport.com

To order your free annual credit report by telephone: call toll-free: 1-877-322-8228

On the web: visit https://www.annualcreditreport.com
By mail: Mail your completed Annual Credit Report Request Form which you can obtain from the Federal Trade Commission's web site at https://www.ftc.gov/bcp/conline/include/requestformfinal.pdf

In writing to:
Annual Credit Report Request Service
P.O. Box 105281
Atlanta, GA 30348-5281

This does not include a free credit score. There are many ways that you can obtain your scores. You can purchase your scores from a score provider such as FreeCreditScore.

com, myFICO, or any of the "Big Three" (Experian, TransUnion, Equifax). There are many companies that will allow you to obtain your report and scores for free, if you sign up for their credit monitoring and pay a monthly fee. There is usually nothing "free" about their services. If you are completing an application for a mortgage or lease, please note that it may be mandatory for the lender or leasing agent to run their own credit report on you.

The lender, bank or broker may be restricted to a tri-merged report. A tri-merge report combines all data and scores from Experian, Trans Union, and Equifax all on one report and includes all three credit scores. Anytime a specific type of report is needed, they usually will run their own and not accept one that you can provide. However, this does not stop you from running your own credit report, for FREE, once every 12 months.

How To Read Your Credit Report

It is no secret that the information on your credit report is very important. But now that you know how to get a credit report, how do you go about reading it? There is a lot of data hidden within the report. There is not a single format used, so it makes it a bit tougher to explain. But let's take it one step at a time. All the steps are relevant. Even if the report you receive varies a little bit, this information is on the report. I am going to go step by step in not only helping you understand what you looking at, but what you are looking for. You should be verifying that all information on all three credit bureaus is correct. You should be prepared to dispute or request correction of any items that are reported in error or have any variances. Your credit report should be a true and accurate view of your credit history.

Step 1 – you will find your name and personal data at the top of page one. You should always make sure that the way your name shows on your report is your legal name. There is no place for nicknames or initials on a credit report. Your address should be your most current, full address including any unit or apartment numbers and zip code. Just one incorrect piece of data, it could create issues for you later. Every time someone runs your credit report with a variance of your legal name you will have these variances shown on future reports. They will show as "also known as" or AKA. For an example: if you are known as Charlie Smith, but your legal name is Charles Michael Smith, unless you identify yourself as Charles or provide a copy of your Driver's License or Social Security card before they run the credit report, you will probably see the name Charlie Smith as one of your AKA's. Aliases will not change your credit score, but can create challenges and extra questions when applying for credit or a job.

Step 2 – Check to make sure that your personal Social Security number is correct. After all we are only human and errors happen. If two numbers get transposed or someone accidently placed your spouse's Social Security number in where your number belonged, your report will have errors or may not be able to supply information at all. If something like this happens, and it does, you will need to notify all three credit reporting bureaus so that this error gets corrected. I suggest you do this immediately.

Step 3 – Your creditors should be listed in the far left column. Normally, the name of the creditor will come first and the account number just below the creditor's name. It is common that the full account number does not show on the report. There should be enough digits of your account number to determine if it is yours or not. Normally you will see all but the last 4-digits of your account number on the report. How ironic, since most paper bills now only show the last 4-digits of the account and if you call for customer care they commonly ask for the last 4-digits of your account number and social before they will talk to you.

If you run your finger to the right of the creditor's name you should find your credit limit, credit balance and then your payment history. Your credit limit is the dollar amount the lending institution has approved for you as the maximum amount you can borrow. Your credit balance is the current balance you owe to the creditor. Your payment history shows whether or not you have paid your obligation on time. If you have been late, the creditor should show the month and year of each late payment. They are usually shown from the most recent late payment to the oldest date. Most creditors will only show going back thirty-six months. I recommend you look at any reported late payment very carefully. If a creditor reports you thirty days late and you know that the payment was made on the twenty-sixth day of the month, they cannot legally report you as late on your credit report. Find and review your payment documentation. If the documentation confirms that it was not thirty days late, consider disputing this account.

Most credit reports will start with paid as agreed accounts (your good credit) and then they will lump together your derogatory accounts. This should make the report a little easier to read, especially if you are trying to clean your credit report.

Step 4 – Public records is anything that has been recorded against you and is available for public access. This section can include, but is not limited to, bankruptcies, judgments, tax liens and even child support liens. These negative items on a credit report can create a huge drop in your credit score. Review them very thoroughly. Everyone wants to have negative items like these removed from their credit report. What if the negative item is accurate? If the negative item is accurate it will remain on your report for seven to ten years. However, what if the negative item has some errors? In a case where the credit reporting company had reported any information in error, you have the right to dispute it. Go through the proper disputing process as identified in the next chapter.

The key is to make sure all you remove erroneous, out of date and unverifiable information from your credit report. Review it thoroughly and make sure it is accurate and complete.

How To Dispute And To Whom

You have a right to dispute any inaccurate information in your credit report. Both the credit reporting bureau and the creditor are responsible for correcting inaccurate or incomplete information in your report once you bring it to their attention. If you find mistakes on your credit report, such as incorrect balances, payment amounts, dates, misspellings, or late payments you should notify the credit reporting company, in writing, with the information you think is inaccurate. It is advised to do this in writing; you can find a sample dispute letter at https://www.consumer.ftc.gov. Your letter should clearly identify each item in your report you wish to dispute. Explain why you are disputing the information and ask that it be removed or corrected. Include copies (originals are not necessary) of documents that support your claim. You may want to enclose a copy of your report with the items in question circled. Send your letter by certified mail, "return receipt requested," so you can document that the credit reporting company received it. Send a second copy to the creditor or information provider letting them know that you are disputing an item on your report. You can use the address provided on your most recent bill or call their customer care department for the address. Keep copies of everything for your records. Credit bureaus must investigate the disputed items usually within thirty days, unless they consider your dispute frivolous.

They also must forward all the relevant documentation you provide about the inaccurate information to the provider, which reviews the information, investigates, and reports the results back to the credit reporting company (or credit bureau). If the information provider finds the disputed information is inaccurate, it must notify all three nationwide credit reporting companies (the "Big Three") so that they can correct the information in your file.

When the investigation is complete, the credit reporting company must give you the result in writing and a free copy of your credit report if the dispute results in a change. If an item is changed or deleted, the credit reporting company cannot put the disputed information back in your file unless the information provider verifies that it is accurate and complete. The credit reporting company also must send you written notice that includes the name, address, and phone number of the information provider.

If you ask, the credit reporting company must send notices of any corrections to anyone who received your report in the past six months. You can have a corrected copy of your report sent to anyone who received a copy during the past two years for employment purposes.

If the investigation doesn't resolve and the disputed item remains on the report, you can request that a statement of the dispute be included in your file and in future reports. You also can ask the credit reporting company to provide your statement to anyone who received a copy of your report in the recent past. There is a fee for this service.

If the dispute process sounds extensive with lots of follow up, you are not seeing the big picture. If writing a letter, mailing it through certified mail, and having incorrect or derogatory items removed from your credit report do not seem worth it, think again. If your credit score only increases a little, it is a step in the right direction. But what after putting in a little effort, it increases a lot? A better credit score will allow you to get better rates on credit cards, mortgages and auto loans. This could save you thousands of dollars in the first year. Don't fight it; life is better with good credit.

> Real Life Scenario - DISPUTE
>
> *I had a client who wanted to refinance their home. We went through the pre-qualifying process together. I showed them that the savings in their mortgage payment would not be substantial due to their high closing costs and add-ons due to low credit scores combined with their loan to value (LTV). We reviewed their credit report together and identified that there were many errors on the report. They seemed minor, but when they disputed the errors, and had the report corrected, their credit scores had increased from 682 to 741. It was enough of an increase in credit score to afford them a better rate for their refinance and better closing costs. Their $395,000 refinance provided them a savings of $518 a month. That is a savings of $6,216 a year and $186,480 over thirty years**
>
> **Savings is based on a 30 year Conventional loan with no PMI. Savings and credit scores are for example only. No APR shown.*

What could you do with another $518 a month or $6,216 a year? How many debts can you start paying down or off? How many nasty phone calls might having these funds available avoid? The rewards are well worth the little work and follow up you put in. The stress usually comes when you spend hours and hours on the phone with a customer care agent who really doesn't care. It may be faster on those occasions where you catch errors on a monthly bill, but not when it has made it to your credit report. I recommend disputing things on your credit report in writing.

How To Spot Identity Theft

In today's criminal world there are always going to be people that will hack into computers, that is a given fact. What are they looking for? In most cases it is data. Your social security number, account information, date of birth, whatever they can get. Your personal information is valuable. They sell it like a car salesperson sells cars. It's what they do. There is a huge market for this information. The more information they extract, the higher the price they get for it. Who buys this information? Marketing companies mostly. The more information on you they have the more stuff they can target and sell you. Are these computer hackers pulling money from our bank or savings accounts? Not usually. However, there are some real bad guys out there who do use this information to steal, setup fraudulent accounts, or borrow money in your name. Ones that hack into computers with the intent that they will use the data they obtain and personally gain. This is called identity theft. You usually don't know that they have your information until you see your credit card statement or receive a call from your creditor.

You could be held responsible for fraudulent charges made. The federal law limits your liability for unauthorized charges to $50, if you report it to your credit card company within two business days from the date you learned about theft or loss. If you wait more than two but less than sixty business days to notify the creditor, you stand to lose up to $500. Wait over sixty business days and you can be responsible for the entire fraudulent charge. The sky's the limit. No room for procrastination here my friends. Report lost/stolen cards or suspicious credit card activity immediately.

If a creditor sees suspicious activity on your account they may be prompted to call you and inquire. They have been known to question consumers and make them feel guilty of a crime. Creditor associates are trained to leave no rock unturned. They may ask if you left your card somewhere, did you allow someone to borrower your card or when was the last time you saw your card. The creditor usually won't just come out and say why the account looks suspicious. They may want to know how you made a purchase for gas in your local community for $45 and purchased a living room set, at the same time, in a different state, on the same day with the same credit card. It is good that the credit card companies are catching these anomalies, but do they really have to treat their card holders like criminals? I have found that some credit card companies are getting better at their "people friendly" skills and are realizing that their customers are all susceptable to being victims of credit card fraud and identity theft.

Here are a few steps to limit your chances of a thief stealing your debit or card information:

1. Only shop on-line from sites you know and trust. Make sure the URL starts with https.

2. Check your account information on-line to look for suspicious transaction(s).
3. Do not leave your PIN number in your wallet (the same place as your ATM card).
4. Leave cards that you do not normally use at home in a safe place.
5. As soon as you receive your statement, review it. Report any discrepancies immediately.
6. Be leery of ATMs that look like they have been tampered with. Look around to see if anyone is lingering. Always be safe. Don't get out of the car if things look suspicious. Move on to the next ATM.
7. Do not place on-line orders from a public Wi-Fi. A hacker can easily intercept your card information.
8. Only give out your credit card information to people you call, not people who call you.

What happens if you do all the right things but you still found an unexplainable charge on your most recent credit card bill? According to the Federal Trade Commission (FTC) you should take these three steps any time you are a victim of fraud.

- Call your bank, credit union or credit card company customer services department and report the fraudulent transaction immediately.
- Follow-up with a paper letter sent through the United States Postal Service to document your report. Include notes of what you discussed on the phone, such as the date, time of day you called and the

name of the person you spoke with. Keep copies of all correspondences.
- Keep your notes and copies of your letters in a separate file. Hang onto this file for several years in case an issue arises later regarding this fraud.

Don't depend on credit card loss protection insurance. Such insurance is not necessary and is considered worthless by the FTC. The credit and debit card loss limits are set by The Fair Credit Billing Act (FCBA) and the Electronic Fund Transfer Act (EFTA). You can obtain more detailed information about your rights by checking out their websites. If you have been a victim, you may want to consider a credit freeze. This is also known as a security freeze. It lets you restrict access to your credit report, which in turn makes it more difficult for identity thieves to open new accounts in your name. Most creditors need to look at your credit report before approving a new account. If they can't see your file they may not extend the credit. You may want to place a credit freeze on your credit reports if you are concerned about the potential consequences of data breaches. To place a credit freeze on your credit reports, you will need to contact each of the nationwide credit reporting companies; Experian, TransUnion and Equifax. There is a small fee of $5 to $10 and you'll need to supply them each with your name, address, date of birth, social security number and other personal information.

A credit freeze does not affect your credit score, prevent you from getting your free annual credit report, keep you from opening new accounts or prevent a thief from incurring charges on your existing accounts. You still need to monitor all bank, credit card and statements for any fraudulent transactions.

(IMAGE COURTESY OF STUART MILES AT FREEDIGITALPHOTOS.NET)

How Long Will Negative Marks Stay On My Report

Each negative mark will stay on your credit report for different lengths of time. Generally, a credit reporting company can report most accurate negative information for seven years. A bankruptcy can show on your credit report for up to ten years. A thirty day late payment may stay on your report for years, but the normal length of time is three years. Most credit trades report up to thirty-six months at a time. There is no time limit on reporting information about criminal convictions; information reported in response to your application for a job that pays more than $75,000 a year; and information reported because you have applied for more than $150,000 worth of credit or life insurance. A judgment against you can be reported for seven years or until the statute of limitations runs out, whichever is longer. Negative items reported are bad for your score. As time passes and they disappear from your report, your credit score will start to rise. Be patient and change will happen with time.

Are you considering purchasing another home after a Foreclosure, Short Sale or Deed in Lieu? Are you trying to refinance or purchase a home after a Bankruptcy? With over 25 years of Real Estate and Lending experience, I have assisted many clients who have asked the same questions.

Do not feel alone, there are a high percentage of people who go through these challenges.

Below are the waiting periods for those of you who have encountered either a Short Sale, Deed in Lieu, Bankruptcy Chapter 7 or Bankruptcy Chapter 13. The chart below will identify how long you have to wait prior to a new purchase or refinance.

Buying a Home After...	Fore-closure	Short Sale	Deed in Lieu	Bankruptcy Chapter 7	Bankruptcy Chapter 13
Conv. Fannie Mae Loan	7yrs from completion date	4yrs from completion date	4yrs from completion date	4yrs from discharge or dismissal date	2yrs from discharge date 4yrs from dismissal date
Conv. Freddie Mac Loan	7yrs from completion date	4yrs from completion date	4yrs from completion date	4yrs from discharge or dismissal date	2yrs from discharge date 4yrs from dismissal date
FHA Loan	3yrs from completion 0-1yrs with extenuating circumstances	3yrs from completion date 0-1yrs with extenuating circumstances	3yrs form completion date 0-1yrs with extenuating circumstances	2yrs from discharge date 1yr with extenuate-ing circum-stances	1yr of the payout must be complete and payment history satisfactory: Buyer must receive Permission from court to enter into a mortgage
VA Loan	2yrs from completion date	No waiting period	2yrs from completion date	2yrs from discharge date	1yr of the payout must be complete and payment history satisfactory: Buyer must receive Permission from court to enter into mortgage

BUYING A HOME AFTER A BANKRUPTCY, FORECLOSURE, OR SHORT SALE: WAITING PERIOD

Stategic Planning To Maintain An Already Good Score

A good score would be one that would afford you the best rates and terms on services, lines of credit and goods. As defined earlier, a credit score between 740 and 850 is the ultimate goal. To obtain that, and maintain it, takes work and planning. If you are currently in this category, you made a lot of very good choices in your repayments of any and all debt. Your goal will be to maintain that excellent payment record. You will need to stay living within your means by way of a budget. Avoid maxing out your credit cards. Only open new lines of credit if and when necessary. Your credit score will usually maintain itself and not decrease as long as you are making your payments on time.

For those who want to be over an 800 score (for bragging rights), but you are just under, you should look a bit harder at your utilization. Most consumers forget that if you owe high balances on your credit cards, even if you pay the minimum payment every month on time, you put your credit score at jeopardy of being weak. Remember, 30% of your credit score is made up of how much you owe and your utilization. Consider getting to a place where you can pay off credit card debt in full at the end of every month. I agree it is ridiculous that you were approved for a credit balance of $5,000 but you should only be using $2,500 or less. Why?

Anything over a 50% utilization rate could reduce your credit score. If you are utilizing more than about 50% of your credit line, it is rated differently than if you have a zero balance. It could be worse, you could be in a position that you need to use that credit line and the balance increases from $2,500 to $5,000 in one given month. In this case your credit score would have a much greater decrease because you are now maxing out the line of credit.

If you currently have "good" credit, identified as credit scores between 680 and 739, and strive to increase it, you should follow the basic steps; make every payment on time or early, do not close good standing accounts, even if you are not using them and watch your utilization on credit cards. Notify data furnishers and credit bureaus to remove any erroneous, out of date and unverifiable information from your credit report. Making payments early or even an extra payment in a given month, when you can afford it, will help maintain your score or even increase it. The combination of good payment habits, with the passing of time from any late payments or derogatory marks on your credit, will continue to make your score increase little by little each month. Follow these tips and you are on your way to excellent credit.

Is Monitoring For Me

Monitoring your credit report is something I feel everyone should do. You can do this on your own by using the FREE Annual Credit Report. As mentioned in the chapter on "How to Get Your FREE Credit Report," you can receive a copy of your credit report for free from Experian, TransUnion and Equifax one time per year from each credit reporting agency. The reports do not all have to be run at the same time. To monitor your reports yourself, I recommend running one bureau every 4 months. You will have a clear picture of your credit worthiness, any changes, fraud or incorrect reporting by doing this. Remember to address anything that is out of the norm to both, the creditor/lender and the credit reporting bureaus, as soon as possible. You do not want to let time pass and possibly become liable for something that is not your responsibility. Follow all the same disputing tactics that are outlined in the heading "How to Dispute and to Whom." Some consumers prefer to pay for the service and purchase credit monitoring service on a monthly basis. This service usually costs around ten to twenty-five dollars a month. These services offer identity theft insurance and compensation if your identity is stolen. Most credit monitoring services will provide you notifications when a new line of credit or new account is opened. Monitoring companies will also notify you if they see unusual activity. You will still be able to check your credit for free annually.

There have been some large commercial companies that have had "security breaches" and offer to pay for your credit to be monitored if you have had your credit compromised. They usually limit the monitoring term of one year, but that is an offer you shouldn't refuse. Currently companies like Discover Card are providing a FICO score on your monthly statement. But who's FICO score? If you have a joint account and want to know who's score is the one shown on the monthly statement, call their customer care department. I have found that in most cases it is the primary card holder.

If you are considering purchasing a subscription to a credit monitoring service, here are a few items to keep in mind;

- Cost is between ten and twenty-five dollars a month
- You can check your credit report frequently without damaging your credit
- You may like monitoring if you have been a victim of identity theft more than once in the previous 12 months
- Monitoring could help you discover why you have been turned down for credit or have had an increase in interest rates on your current lines of credit if you are not sure why.

I feel that credit monitoring is a must for all consumers. However, paying money for a credit monitoring service is a personal preference. Knowing what is on our report and monitoring this is something each of us can do for free, by using the annual free credit reports we get from all the "Big Three" (Experian, TransUnion, Equifax). However, if you feel you need to have a service to assist you in this task, you should budget for it and subscribe.

CHAPTER 3:

Increasing Your Credit Score Made Easy

Simple Steps To Improve Your Credit Score

There are some simple steps to improving your credit score. However, don't view credit improvement like a race. It takes time and patience. I like the analogy that a credit score is not like a race car, where you can rev the engine and almost instantly feel the result. It is more like your driving record: They take into account years of past behavior, not just your present actions. Good, bad or ugly, there are numerous types of credit. I am going to simplify this into five categories. Find the one category that matches you the best. It won't be perfect, but once you identify with one of the categories, I can best help you improve your credit score. Pick the category that best represents your current situation. Go with your worst case scenario. For example; if you have a thirty day late on your VISA card, a collection account with Best Buy and sold your home in a Short Sale two years ago, you would be in Category 1 because the Short Sale would be the most derogatory mark on your credit report. Choose one of the following:

Category 1 – I have claimed bankruptcy, have judgment(s), tax liens or defaulted on a home (this includes short sale, deed in lieu and modifications) or auto loan within the last 5 years.

Category 2 – I have collection accounts, charge offs or reported back child support

Category 3 – I have been 30 days late on more than one of my credit obligations within the past 2 years.

Category 4 – I have fewer than 4 credit trade lines or I am new to credit.

Category 5 – I have over-all good credit and/or I have lots of credit. I pay my bills on time, but my credit score isn't as high as I think it should or could be.

Now that you know where you land, we can start working on increasing your credit score. **Category 1** – If this best describes your current credit situation, then we have some work to do. Since we can't go backwards, let's take small steps toward moving forward. It is back to basics with those of you who have claimed bankruptcy, have judgment(s), tax liens or defaulted on a home and/or auto loan within the last five years.

Once a bankruptcy is on your report it will remain on your credit up to ten years. Work on other ways to increase your score. Once the bankruptcy is discharged, you can start considering the steps to re-establish good credit trades. Consider a secured card at first. A bankruptcy is not a death sentence. FHA can approve a home loan just two years out of bankruptcy with a minimum credit score and re-established credit. Two years is not that long a wait.

`When it comes to judgments and tax liens, you should definitely consider the art of negotiation. I have seen many successful cases of "pennies on the dollar" pay offs and the savings are well worth the effort, especially when you consider the high rate of interest. If you have a tax lien, I recommend you address it immediately, if you haven't already. Unlike a bankruptcy and judgments, tax liens don't have a set time during which they will just fall off of your credit report. Make a plan and budget for it. Request a payments program that fits your budget. Don't be scared, average people negotiate affordable terms every day. You don't need to pay thousands to a lawyer or credit-fix-it company to accomplish this. Don't let the lien holder have you commit to something you know you cannot pay. You have to hold your ground and let them know if the payments they propose will be a hardship for you. In most cases, they do want to work with you. Note that the balance they say you owe may be different than what you calculated. They may have included late payments, high interest, and penalties to the balance owed. These should also be negotiated.

Short Sales, Deeds in Lieu and Judgments will stay on your credit for up to seven years. Like a bankruptcy, time passes while those derogatory marks get further and further away. This allows your credit scores to rise. Short Sales and Modifications create a negative mark on your credit and have more weight than a credit card or auto loan. Your mortgage is usually the largest credit line established. To pay a bank less than owed, like in a short sale or to change the originally agreed on terms, like in a modification, damages the credit score drastically. There is no set number by which the credit score will decrease, but it is always damaging.

As bad as things may seem, there is light at the end of the credit tunnel. Start off small again. Don't go back to drowning yourself in debt. New lines of credit you open should be manageable. There is no crime in getting a credit card with a low limit. People who get credit cards with $500 credit limits can achieve the same high credit scores as those with $10,000 credit limits. You can build it up over time. You can request to negotiate balances and/or payments on any open credit card to make things more affordable. This is true of most creditors. They will allow you to adjust your payments or negotiate balances in order not to default. Remember, this is not a race. Credit scores will increase over time. Be patient and don't be tempted to change course once you start heading in the right direction.

Category 2 – Collection accounts, charge offs and back child support are no laughing matters. They tell a story to a prospective creditor that you have not paid your past credit obligations and that you may not be a good credit risk. It is time to change the stigma and turn things around. A collection account is a creditor or a third party trying to collect a debt that you did not or could not pay. You can do one of several things with a collection account; pay the debt in full, negotiate the pay-off of the debt or dispute the debt. Disputing is usually done if there is more than one creditor trying to collect for the same debt and you think the information varies. Address each account separately. It is always best to try and negotiate with the originator of the debt first. For example, if ABC Collection Company is collecting a debt on behalf of Dr. William Smith for an unpaid medical bill. You should try to negotiate a payoff with Dr. Smith and request that Dr. Smith notify ABC Collection Company, who is collecting on his behalf, to report the debt as paid and to cease contacting you regarding the account. You should also submit copies of the paid in full paperwork to ABC Collection Company and all three credit bureaus requesting they report the paid status. The rating will now show that you have paid that obligation.

Charge offs are filed when a creditor has tried to collect a debt, is unsuccessful and removes the debt off their books. Even after the company charges the debt off their books, they may still employ a collection agency to collect the debt or any portion thereof to mitigate their losses. Unless a creditor is coming after you in collections, I would place this debt lower on the priority list of debtors to pay. It will just sit on the credit report for seven years as a derogatory mark whether it is unpaid or paid. Charge offs are still a debt and you may choose to negotiate this debt if you have the liquidity to do so but it will show as a paid charge off and still stay on your report as a negative mark for seven years unless during your negotiations you offer payment for removal of the debt from your report.

Social Services send credit bureaus a monthly list of parents who are more than $1,000 behind on child support payments. The reporting continues as long as payments are due on a child support case. If you make arrangements and pay back child support (also known as child support arrearages) and still owe current child support, your account will still be reported, but will now reflect a zero balance past due. Even after you pay off the arrearages, the negative information can stay on your report for years, but your score will increase over time. You can request payments for child support to be modified by court order so that you can budget and pay arrearages off with current payments, if needed. Don't ignore the many ways that Social Services can recover back child support, including the garnishing of wages. Try to be proactive in letting the courts know what you can do to resolve the issue. Your goodwill will go a long way.

Category 3 – If you have been late on more than one of your credit obligations within the past two years, time is going to be your best friend. A late payment will eventually drop off as time passes. As long as you are now paying on time and continue to pay on time, your score will increase. Your goal is to pay everything on time from here forward. Every time you make a late payment, there is more damage and the clock resets. It may be time for you to set up auto pay and stop being late. Remember, a creditor can only report you as late to the credit reporting bureaus if your payment is thirty days late or greater. Let's say that your payment is due on the first of the month. You know that the creditor received the payment on the 27th and posted the payment on the 29th of the month, they cannot report you as thirty days late. This will negatively impact your credit score. You may have to pay a late fee and additional interest, but you should not be reported as late. In this case, you should send copies of your paid documentation (receipts, cancelled checks or on-line statement) with a dispute letter requesting the thirty day late be removed immediately.

Category 4 – If you are new to credit, only have a few lines of credit or feel uncomfortable about having a monthly payment, it only takes about three lines of credit to create a credit score. You are not required to have rolling credit balances. The credit pros will only charge what they can afford to pay off at the end of every month. Are you scared to open a credit card for fear you will abuse it? Consider applying for a department store or gas card with a credit limit of $250. This will still initiate a line of credit being reported to all three credit reporting bureaus and provide you a credit limit that is manageable. Once you get a handle on one card, you'll be on your way to establishing additional accounts, as you need them.

For those of you who already have a few lines of credit, you want to take baby steps. If you have three or four accounts, you don't need to add credit cards just to have more credit. You should start focusing on what type of credit you do have. If the three or four lines of credit consist of a mortgage, an auto loan, a Visa and a Chevron card, you did it! You have a solid variety of credit. If you make your payments on time, every month, you have the makings of an excellent credit score. However, if you have four lines of credit and they are all revolving cards (a mix of department stores and gas stations) with limits of $500 and under, you just don't have the diversity or credit balances that usually get the scores up as high. If you are ready for the next step, consider increasing the credit limits on the cards you already have. Next time you are ready to buy a car, consider financing options. Only finance what your budget will allow, not what the salesman will say you may qualify for.

If you open a new Visa, request the credit limit be the maximum that they will allow (this is usually based on your current credit and income). Your goal is to never max out a card but to use no more than 50% of the credit limit. Continue these baby steps until you achieve your goals. Keep yourself in check every step of the way. Don't walk too fast. If you stumble, it will cost you big. I would rather see you stick with a solid credit score of 620 to 720 with only a few store credit cards than over extend yourself. Incur just one late payment and you could be dragged down to credit scores between 588 and 599. Stay focused my friend.

Category 5- If you make your payments on time, but are only making the minimum payment on revolving debt month after month and you feel like you are not getting anywhere, you should consider paying balances off. Start with the cards with the lowest balances. We refer to those small balances on numerous cards as nuisance balances. A great way to increase your credit score is to budget and eliminate the nuisance balances as soon as possible. How can this help your score? FICO considers just how many of your cards have balances. So, when you charge $95 on one card and $45 on another, instead of using the same card, it can negatively affect your score. To meet your new goals, evaluate the cards that you do have; credit limit, interest rate and terms (this can include cash back and frequent flyer miles). Keep two cards that can handle your spending habits that have the best rates and terms, gather all the other credit cards that you have small balances on and pay them off.

Remember, even if you pay off balances in full every month, you could still have a higher utilization ratio than you'd expect. This is because some creditors use the balance on your statement as the one reported to the "Big Three" credit bureaus. Even if you are paying off balances in full every month, your credit score could still reflect your monthly charges.

Another strategy is to see if the credit card company will accept multiple payments throughout the month. Let's say your payment is due on the 1st and you make the minimum payment. You get paid again on the 15th of the same month and make another payment for $50 toward principle only (you already paid that month required interest in the minimum payment on the 1st). This can help pay off the card faster and improve your credit score at the same time.

Now, what do you do with the credit cards you just paid off? Good credit paid off is still good credit. Leave it alone! One of the ways to improve your score is to leave the old debt and good accounts on as long as possible. You want to do this anytime you have a good repayment record.

Do not immediately have a cut-it-up party, but do not carry credit cards that you are not intending to use in your wallet. Put them in a sock drawer at home and don't use them. The longer your history of good debt is, the better it is for your score.

How To Negotiate Debt

If you pay a debt in collections in full, you will be obligated to paying the principle, interest charges (usually at high rates), with late fees, where applicable, and possibly attorney's fees. Negotiating the debt is a much better option. Build up a reserve of about fifty to sixty percent of the debt, then call to negotiate. This is a common practice with collection accounts and charge offs. It is always best to negotiate with the originator of the debt.

Beware of the tough guy tactics. Collectors are trained to collect as much money as they can squeeze out of you. They are known as the "bullies of the play yard." Stay focused on what you want to accomplish, pay as little as possible to get the debt shown as paid or even deleted from your credit report. Have a maximum dollar amount you are willing to negotiate with and stick to your guns. Do not let them bully you into giving them a credit card over the phone to pay the balance. Remember, they only care about collecting as much money from you as they can to resolve the debt. They do not care where the funds come from. You should always document who you spoke to, the date and time of your conversation. Write reviewable notes. At the end of the negotiations you should request the creditor show the account as paid or to remove the debt from your credit report.

Being late on your auto loan places you in jeopardy of a repossessed vehicle. For some, this is their only mode of transportation to and from work. Cure delinquent auto payments by asking them to include the delinquent amount on the back of the principle balance and renegotiate new affordable payments.

You will find that almost any creditor is willing to negotiate the debt owed. Getting something is better than getting nothing. What have you got to lose? Remember to have a clear objective when you initiate the call and do not get bullied. Negotiate away my friends.

Real Life Scenario – MEDICAL BILLS/COLLECTIONS

A child fell out of a tree and appeared unconscious. The parents called 911. The emergency vehicles arrived and the boy was brought to the closest emergency room by ambulance. He was diagnosed with a broken arm and a concussion. He was released and asked to follow up with his primary care physician. His mother brought him in to their primary care physician the next day for follow up and the doctor referred her to an outside orthopedic surgeon for her son's arm. After more X-rays, no surgery was needed. He was going to be fine after being in a cast for six to eight weeks. About three weeks after the incident, the family started to receive numerous medical bills. They were sure that their medical insurance would cover all their expenses, after all it was an emergency. Bill after bill came rolling in. Emergency room costs, ambulance, x-ray technicians, doctors and more. As the bills came in, the mother called each service provider to assure them that her medical insurance should be paying their claim. She spent hours on the phone with the medical insurance company trying to get things squared away. Months pass and more bills. It was a nightmare. She thought she finally had everything under control. She thought that the insurance company had paid all claims. Six months later she received collection account threats from a third party collection agency. When she called to inquire further, she found out that the collection company was collecting the debt for the orthopedic surgeon. The insurance company had not paid his claim. The mom got back on the phone with the insurance company and asked them to pay the orthopedic bill and that they were threatening her with collections. Assuming that the doctor would be paid, she put it behind her.

Months later she was declined for a credit card she applied for. When she asked why, she was told it was due to the most recent unpaid collection. With more phone calls to the collection account and the insurance company, she found out that the orthopedic surgeon that she was referred to by her primary care physician was not covered under her plan. She was livid. The collection account remained on her credit report unpaid until she had the funds to negotiate it and paid it off a year later.

How Many Lines Of Credit Should I Have

There is no set number reflecting the lines of credit one should or should not have. Each person is as individual as their finger print. For a consumer to rate a credit score, the credit bureaus are looking for a minimum of three credit trades to reasonably form enough data to provide a credit rating or FICO score. Once you have provided enough data for your credit scores to be formed, your goal will be to do everything you can to improve your credit score and maintain an excellent rating.

Instead of considering how many lines of credit you should have, you should be asking yourself what types of accounts you should have. If you have established two or three lines of credit and are looking to open another credit card account, look carefully at what the card offers. Does it have an annual fee? Will they waive the annual fee for the first year? Are they offering a zero interest rate for the first six months? You should be planning ahead. Budget for when there is an annual fee or continue looking for a card that has no annual fee. What will the interest rate be after the first six months? Do not assume you might get another offer with zero interest as this card changes from zero to twenty-nine percent. It may not happen and you will be stuck paying twenty-nine percent interest.

Mortgages and auto loans hold higher weight to credit scores. Keeping a diverse credit report with a variety of accounts is important also. A mortgage, an auto payment, a VISA and a MasterCard is a great line up in the credit world.

It is not always how much credit you have, as it is making sure each account on my credit report is optimized. Watch those credit card balances. One of the best ways to boost your score is to "pay down balances." Great rule of thumb; do not let your credit card balance go higher than fifty percent of the credit limit on the card. If you really want to optimize your results, bring the credit card balances to ten percent of the credit limit. This is not always possible, but for those who can, do it. Also, the balance of a revolving account can be paid in full every month and still have great credit optimization.

Make multiple payments throughout the month. Always make the minimum monthly payment on or before they are due, but make a second payment within the same billing cycle if and when possible. Once you structure a budget for this, it will be easier.

Julie Marie McDonough

On-Line Bill Paying

Most Americans are now paying their bills electronically. A click here, a click there and it's like magic; you have paid your bill. It is a simple process, painless and paperless. Everyone is going "green". Since a late or missed payment can negatively affect your credit score, online bill paying is a great free tool to help you stay on track to better credit. The majority of creditors allow you to sign up for online billing. You can instruct them to email you your monthly statement and alert you when a bill is coming due or becomes past due. Automatic monthly payment options will allow you to choose a date on which to have payments automatically withdrawn from your personal bank account every month. You can also use different payment options to meet your personal needs. If you have been afraid to try on line bill paying because of identity theft or fraud, it is no larger risk than if you buy a pair of theatre tickets online. Most online payment processing companies have secured sites and extra firewalls.

I highly recommend that if you pay your bills online that you are checking your account online too? For every click to pay a bill, you should click one more time and make sure that the payment you just made posted to your account. Always check your account status. Make sure that the last payment you made is error free. Catching errors and getting them corrected immediately will save you time and money in the long run. Automation is a great way to ensure that you will never miss a scheduled payment. You and your credit report will be glad you did.

CREDIT MYTHS

- **If you make a lot of money, own houses, boats, fancy cars and jets, you must have great credit.**

  Rich people can have bad credit just like anyone else.

- **Credit activity from all creditors is reported on the first day of every month.**

  Each creditor reports activity once a month, but it does not necessarily have to be on the first day of each month.

- **I can consolidate my credit cards and hide debt.**

  Sorry, the debt is not hidden; it is just divided over more than one credit card. This is all very visible on a credit report and may back fire.

- **Paying cash for everything will help my credit rating.**

  This is not true since cash payments are not reflected in your credit rating and good payment history will not be acknowledged. Consider using a Visa or M/C for small purchases and paying them off in full at the end of the billing cycle.

- **If a consumer fails to pay a bill because he/she feels that the bill was incorrect, the consumer is not responsible.**

The consumer is obligated to pay the debt. If he/she feels that the bill is incorrect, for any reason, you must work with the creditor to get it corrected. If the creditor is in error, they will credit you for any overages proven.

- **Paying off all accounts and closing them will help my credit rating.**

You should always keep good credit accounts open for as long as possible, even if you are not using them.

- **Once I pay off a credit card to zero balance, the item will be removed from my credit report immediately.**

A credit card paid to a zero balance can still show as an open account with a zero balance on your credit report. The line of credit is still available for use unless you close the account. Delinquent accounts can continue to show on your report for up to seven years.

- **There is only one credit score.**

There are a total of three credit scores, one from each of the major credit reporting bureaus (Experian, TransUnion and Equifax).

Be Diligent and Don't Give Up

A bad credit score can really put a damper on things. It can limit your financial options and adds an extra layer of stress to your life. In order to improve your credit score, you may have to revise your spending habits and stay within your budget. No matter what type of credit you have today, you must realize that rebuilding your credit score will take some time. But, in the end, you have an opportunity to change "denied" to "approved." You can be approved for the best possible rates and terms on home and auto loans, credit cards and more. So how much time is this going to take? Realistically, someone with bad credit, even a bankruptcy, can expect the proper steps taking a couple of years to build a good credit rating.

Let's take a look at what you need to do:

- Be diligent and don't give up
- Don't miss payments
- Reduce debt

Be diligent. Schedule some time to identify bills you can pay off and how fast. Be realistic on your timeline. It makes more sense to make small steps and succeed than to try to leap and fail. It is an incremental building block process. Think of it as rebuilding a falling building. You have to evaluate, redesign and rebuild. When your credit is damaged, it can affect different facets of your life. It will become frustrating at times and it takes patience. Don't give up. By dealing with bad credit correctly, you can improve the quality of your life.

Do not miss payments. Auto pay is the greatest tool for those of you who know when you get paid, have the funds in the bank, but just have so much stuff going on in your life that you forget to pay your bills on time. Here is a great tip for many of you; a payment that is made after the due date but received by the creditor before it is thirty days late, cannot be shown on a credit report as a late payment. You may have to pay a late charge or even additional interest, but do not let your accounts become late thirty days or beyond. Just one thirty day late payment on your credit report can have a significant negative effect on your credit score.

If you have sold your property in a short sale, getting back into being a homeowner is a bit more challenging. Fannie Mae and Freddie Mac have a "waiting period" before you can purchase a home again. It is ok, do not fret, use all the tools taught in the book, increase your credit score, and become a homeowner again with good rates and terms. When you add new credit, along with removing negative accounts, your credit scores should really increase. This is especially true if you are adding new positive revolving credit with good credit limits.

Remember, 35% of the score is based on how you pay your bills and 30% of the total credit score is based on available credit. So when you add positive credit accounts with good limits, you raise your available credit and help improve your overall percentage of paid-as-agreed accounts which in turn increases your credit score.

This is perfect for you because when you add positive new credit with good limits, your scores can be raised even without negative items being deleted. So even if you are struggling to remove negative items from your report, you can still see increases to your scores based on the positive available credit that was added.

Reducing your debt can only be done if you have the liquid assets to pay them down. It is time to reflect on the budget and see where you can cut back in order to have a little extra each month to put toward paying off your debt. It probably took a while to build the debt so it will probably take a while to pay it down. Remember you want to bring the credit limits on your existing credit cards down to approximately 50-60% of the credit limit to optimize your utilization. This is weighted as 30% of your credit score. Do this alone and you can make your score increase. It takes time to budget and pay the debt, but it is totally worth it.

How can I cut back? How often do you go out to dinner and the movies? Cost of an evening out has skyrocketed. If you refrain from one dinner out a month and a movie, your savings could be $75 a month. That's $900 a year! If you like cocktails with dinner it could be a lot more. Eat a nice meal at home and go for a nice walk in the park instead. Put that money toward paying down your debt.

CHAPTER 4:

Building Credit and Budgeting

Living Within Your Means and Learning to Budget

There are a lot of people who do not live within their means. For most of us, this is a difficult task. What does it mean to live within my means? If you are able to pay all your bills and credit cards, in full, at the end of the month, and can put 3-5% of your income in savings, you are living within your means.

If you are not, here is a great rule of thumb to get started moving in that direction. Identify 45% of your gross monthly income (before you pay taxes). For example if you make $5,500.00 a month and times that by .45 (45%), you should get $2,475.00. This amount ($2,475.00) is your new monthly budget. You can spend up to $2,475.00 a month on housing, credit cards, and auto payment. This includes anything that is a monthly payment that will show on your credit report. What doesn't this include; housing utilities, cell phone bill, auto insurance, and items that do not show up on your credit report. This is the same formula used by Fannie Mae, Freddie Mac and FHA to qualify you for a home loan. If you can't get to 45% of your income right away and pay all your bills, don't worry. Make smaller goals to achieve, write them down and make consistent changes to make it happen. Start by prioritizing. Write a list of all your monthly bills. Consider dividing your annual debts by twelve and include them as part of the monthly calculations. Identify which bills you might be able to pay off quickly. Make sure to pay off credit cards that hold high interest rates first. Consider cutting back on things like eating out and movie theaters. Married couples have to consider compromising on where you can cut back. You may also consider improving your education and/or getting a better job to increase your income.

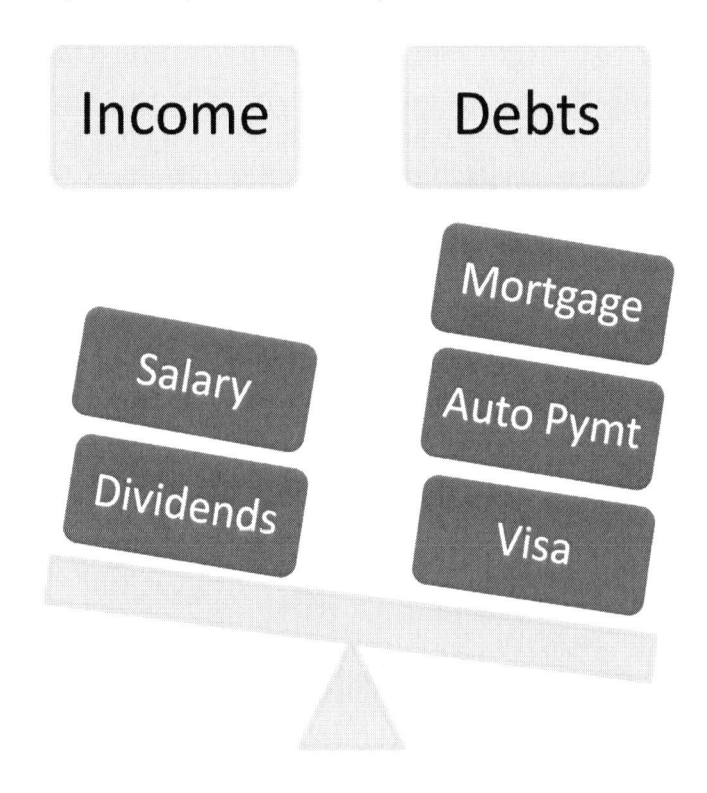

Now that you have a budget (45% of your gross monthly income), you can start modifying current spending habits. Maybe you have a current budget, but you may not have used this formula before. Give it a try. You'll find that you may have to make some changes. For most people, housing is their largest single expense. This will dig pretty heavily into your monthly budget. Once you deduct the housing payment, how much you have left may dictate the type of car or auto payment you can afford, and how much you should be spending on credit cards and other items. If this is one of those "OMG" moments in your life and you just realized that you are spending over 70% of your whole paycheck every month on housing, auto payment(s) and credit card bills, then it is time to make some changes immediately. Remember, our budget is based on gross monthly income (before they take out taxes). If you are in a 25% tax bracket, then you are only bringing home 75% of your gross. For example, if you make $5,500.00 a month gross, you are taking home about $4,125.00. Don't kid yourself into thinking that you can squeeze any more out of a salaried paycheck. When you are an hourly employee and your hours change all the time, take a six month average. This will assist in budgeting. Because your income will vary from paycheck to paycheck, you have to be conservative. If you budget using an average and you are in retail, where you will get more hours during peak seasons, put that extra money in the bank. This will help in the weeks and months that you do not quite have enough. Always try to build a reserve account to draw from during leaner times. You do not want to increase your debts during these times, because the money is not going to last.

What kind of budgeting can you do if you are self-employed to protect yourself in slowing economic times? I personally have been self-employed my whole adult life, and I can tell you from experience that it is not always easy. The overhead of running a business is not always consistent while the cost of goods and services may change with the seasons. In my experience, the best way to protect yourself is to be conservative when putting together a budget. Base your income on a two year average (if you are extremely conservative and have been in business over 10 years, use a five year average). This should be done to calculate monthly averages, especially if you are in manufacturing, retail or food services. These industries tend to have trends that are seasonal. For the self-employed who file a Schedule "C" with their taxes, you should be using the income or (loss) from line 21 on your 1040's. Adding back depreciation is usually allowed. Now that you know how to calculate your monthly income, use the same calculations as above. Use 45% of your monthly income to calculate a personal monthly budget.

Now you have an idea of what your new budget will be, are you freaking out just a little? Most are. If you are really serious about putting your financial house in order you have to find a way to live within your means and live on a budget. It may take some time to get there. Don't give up. When you go to buy a house, refinance your current home loan, obtain a line of credit or buy investment property with either Fannie Mae/Freddie Mac, a bank, or FHA you will have to meet these income guidelines to qualify. It is best to know this now and be prepared. It doesn't matter if you are ready for that kind of purchase or just starting to build credit, using these tools for budgeting and living within your means will help.

Are you single? Have you been seeing someone and its getting serious? Are you currently engaged? Have you considered buying a home down the line with that special someone? Make sure you talk about your financial goals and where you are both at with your credit scores. One good credit score does not offset a bad one. Lenders look at the whole picture and usually use the lower of the two middle scores. If you are the individual that has the higher credit score, your purchasing power, when buying something jointly, will be compromised. Help your partner identify a budget using the same formula and take the steps to better credit.

How about those with an overwhelming amount of student debt? This should be something to talk about. You should be upfront and honest with your partner and work together to optimize your creditworthiness. For those of you contemplating student debt, be realistic about the final amount of debt versus what those in your intended major can earn. Student debt will impact your ability to responsibly spend and your debt ratios after graduation.

New Credit Users And Building Credit

There are millions who are literally scared to apply for credit. For most it is the fear of being denied. Be prepared, you may get a couple of no's before you get the "yes." The following tips may help you lose the fear.

Department Store Credit Card; for most of us, a store credit card was our first line of credit. Store credit has been known as the "Training Wheels" of the credit world. You have to start somewhere and this allows you to build small and safe with confidence. With a credit card, a person has the financial ability to make purchases without cash or an ATM card. Learning how to be financially responsible is extremely important. There are a few pros and cons to using store credit cards to build, or even rebuild, your credit history. Department store cards tend to be easier to obtain a credit approval, especially if you have never had a credit card before. The credit limit may start off small, sometimes in the hundreds, thus the risk of running up thousands of dollars in debt is not possible. The balance is manageable and therefore so is the monthly payment. There are other advantages to department store cards; they offer discounts, advanced notices to sales, e-coupons, special shopping times and days, along with other deals that non-card holders will not receive. It makes you feel special.

For all the upsides, there are some downsides as well. If you plan to carry a balance on a store card, you should expect to pay a much higher interest rate than you would with Visa or Master Card. You will generally see interest rates at about 10% to 15% higher on store cards than with Visa or Master Card. Not a huge impact when purchasing a new outfit for work or a swimsuit for the summer season, but it could be hard to handle when considering a large purchase like living room furniture. Don't get in the trap of maxing out your balance on one store card and opening another line of credit at another department store. This can lead you down a self-destructive path. It will work against you if you open a lot of credit lines in a short period of time. Department stores tend to close accounts, especially those that are inactive for long periods of time. This can affect your credit score as well. You should also be aware that some department stores or credit card companies may charge an annual fee.

Another option for consumers trying to establish credit is the Secured Credit Card. With a secured credit card, you place a deposit into a bank account and that deposit "secures" the card for you. The card issuer or bank gives you a credit card that you can use just like a regular credit card. It will have the same appearance as any VISA or Master Card and you can use it almost anywhere. Make sure you get a secured card that reports all credit history to the credit reporting bureaus (Experian, TransUnion and Equifax).

Many consumers, after getting their first card, start getting offers from other creditors. Do not apply for too many cards. You can spiral out of control very quickly. Once you have established the credit lines, it will be your mission to pay all payments on time or early, EVERY TIME. Nothing less is acceptable. We are building your credit score up. We are going to SOAR together in the cloud of 800 plus. One late and you could get grounded to working harder, month after month, to regain your wings. Stay afloat my friends.

Good Credit Habits

- Create a budget and stay within your budget.
- Pay your bills on time, EVERY TIME. Pay ahead of the due date if possible.
- Set up auto pay if you are, at all, unsure you will pay on time.
- Monitor your credit. Always be looking for something out of the norm.
- Know your limitations.
- Shop for the best rates and terms on goods and services.
- Don't feel ashamed to ask questions.
- Read the fine print before you sign.
- Avoid Short-term loans. The high interested rates will put you back.

Your Credit And Real Estate Loan Requests

In the mortgage industry, the goal for obtaining the best rates and terms would be to have a middle credit score of 740 or greater. Why this score? 740 or greater would provide you the best rates and terms with no additional costs or fees to a conventional loan. If your score is below 740, the lending institution sees you as a higher risk, and although your loan may be approved, you would pay an additional fee, called an add-on. Consider a $300,000 mortgage; someone with a score below 740 could end up paying additional costs between $3,000 and $6,000 for the same loan as someone with a middle score of 741 or greater. Please note that the loan-to-value is factored into any add-on. For you to get the best rates and terms for services, you have to know how, not only to bring your score up, but to keep it elevated. This example is based on a purchase with 10% down or a 90% Loan to Value (LTV).

Remember, the credit score range starts at 300 and ends at 850. Whether you have a good score or a bad one, the credit score range will always be within 300 and 850. You should also realize that your score is usually not constant – it will keep changing. For instance, if you have taken a home mortgage, your score will improve with each monthly, on time, repayment. There will be negative consequence if you fail to make the payment on time. In an effort to explain what a bad credit score is verses an excellent credit score, I put together the following score range. The scores tend to correspond with standard approval lending guidelines for the mortgage industry.

Here is a credit score range for comparison purposes:

- **Between 740 and 850 – Very good to excellent credit score.**
- **Between 720 and 739 – Good credit score.**
- **Between 620 and 719 – Average or OK score.**
- **Between 580 and 619 – Low credit score.**
- **Between 500 and 579 – Poor credit score.**
- **Between 300 and 499 – Bad credit score.**

If you have a score around 750, then your application has a much greater chance of being approved than someone with a 580 score. You will get very favorable terms too because you are among the most creditworthy people to any lender. If you are in the 680 to 699 credit score range, then you also can become approved for your loan request, though it might be at a slightly higher rate or additional fees and charges may apply. If your score is somewhere between; 580-619, then it is going to become a little harder for you to get approved for a loan. FHA has programs for borrowers with a score of at least 580, but the terms are going to more costly than if you had better credit. While some lenders may give you the loan, there will be others who might reject your application. Non-institutional lenders and private investment loans are an option, but come with higher rates and fees. You should expect to pay anywhere between one and five percent higher on interest with non-institutional and private lenders. For some, this might be the only option to become a homeowner at the time of distressed credit. Because the terms are not regulated the same as FHA, Fannie Mae or Freddie Mac, I urge you to know what you are getting into. Ask questions until you feel comfortable with the terms. Consider asking if the loan has a balloon payment (fixed for a short term, but then due in payable) or if it has a pre-payment penalty (a costly penalty if you hit the lottery and want to pay the loan off early). Please read everything before you sign it. Never be afraid to ask questions.

People, who fall in the last two categories in the credit score range (300-579), have almost zero chance of getting a standard conventional home loan. Their application is sure to be rejected by almost all institutional lenders. If you fall in either of these categories, it is time for you to focus on what you can do to increase your score, and look forward to homeownership after you have increased your score to 580 or above.

Remember, while the credit score range remains constant, your score will keep changing. If you find that your score is low, hold off on applying for the loan until you feel comfortable with the terms. Try to improve your score and check back after some time. Apply for the loan only when you find that your score has improved. You can go to http://www.amerisell.com and complete the free, no obligation pre-qualification page. This will allow you to find out what you qualify for hassle free.

Tri-Merged Reports

Creditors and lenders run credit reports for one thing, to see if you are a good credit risk. They want to know how likely it is that you will repay the debt. Some creditors, and most mortgage lenders, require a tri-merged credit report to confirm your creditworthiness. A tri-merge report is when one report reflects the data from all of the "Big Three" (Experian, TransUnion and Equifax). This single report will merge all of your credit information into a format that provides an underwriter or reviewer with all your credit data, combined with credit scores, together in one easy to read format. Again, it is not uncommon to have different credit scores from bureau to bureau. Your tri-merged report will reflect all three scores on one report. It is common that a mortgage lender will use the "middle" score for qualifying purposes. For example, your Experian score may be 702, TransUnion 690, and Equifax 725. The lender will base your rates and terms on the middle score which in this example is 702. If you are married, both you and your spouse's credit and scores can be shown together on one tri-merged report. The report will show three scores for each of you, so a total of six scores on this one report. Lenders tend to be conservative and use the lower of the two middle scores (one middle score for each spouse). So even if one of the spouses is currently unemployed or a stay at home mom or dad, your credit is still weighted. This type of report is used sometimes by landlords or management companies with eviction data supplied as well.

Teaching Teens About Credit

A parent is a role model on how a teen will develop. Parents are sometimes the sole source for knowledge when it comes to finance and their credit. What are you teaching your teen through example? By the age of 10 (or earlier for some) a parent should help their child open a "Kids Club" type of account. These are available at most banks and credit unions for FREE. This allows the pre-teen to start managing money, even if it is very little. It doesn't take much to open an account and there are no monthly or annual fees. They will get a bank statement, just like you. You should help them understand their statement and how to balance at the end of the month.

As your pre-teen becomes a teen he or she should be savvy about saving, when they turn 18 years old, they may be ready to start their credit history. If your son or daughter is in their senior year of high school at the age of 18 and applying for colleges, you will probably see that they are getting offers for small credit lines of $250-$500. This is a great start if they learn how to use the credit they are offered. Not unlike their parents, they have to manage their time, money and credit. I find that many of our young adults prefer to do on-line banking and use auto-pay. Using technology to make life easier just makes sense. My son was only 17 when he went off to college. We wanted a way he could pay for college expenses without us putting money in his personal account all the time. One of the ways I did this was to open a new Visa card and add him as a signer. He had all the same signing privileges as I did, but because he was not yet 18 years old, the usage would not rate on his credit report. Once he turned 18, we changed some paperwork and from then forward it reflected as a good credit line on his credit report. This was also a great way to oversee all of the college expenses as they are accrued.

Even if your teen is not looking at college right away it is still possible that they are getting offers as well. But what if they are not and they want to start using credit? Here are a few tips you can share with your teen;

1. Apply for a Visa or MC with the bank you currently do banking with. You have already established a relationship with them from your "Kids Club" account. Banks that have an existing track record are more likely than those who do not.

2. Apply for a department store card. They will offer a low credit limit, but they are more likely to grant first-timers credit. The interest charged on the department store cards is usually high, but if you pay the balance off in-full at the end of every billing cycle, you pay zero interest. The credit card companies are counting on most people not having the discipline to pay the entire balance each month. After six months to a year of making your payments on time, you should be ready to ask the creditor to increase the credit limit.

3. Apply for a gas station card. Every gas station takes Visa, MC, AMEX, Discover, Diner's Club and many more. They are another source of credit with flexible terms for first time credit users.

Co-signing for your teen is a danger zone. Yes, many of us have done it. As I mentioned previously, I had a joint credit card with my son. That meant that, although he was the only one racking up the bill, I was just as obligated to this debt as he was. I had on-line access to the account and I received paper billings monthly. I trusted him, but as all of us should know by now, stuff happens. Trust but verify. Identity theft and lost or stolen cards are just a few things that can happen. If you chose to co-sign for your child, whether they are 18 or 35 years old, you have to be aware of your financial obligations to the debt.

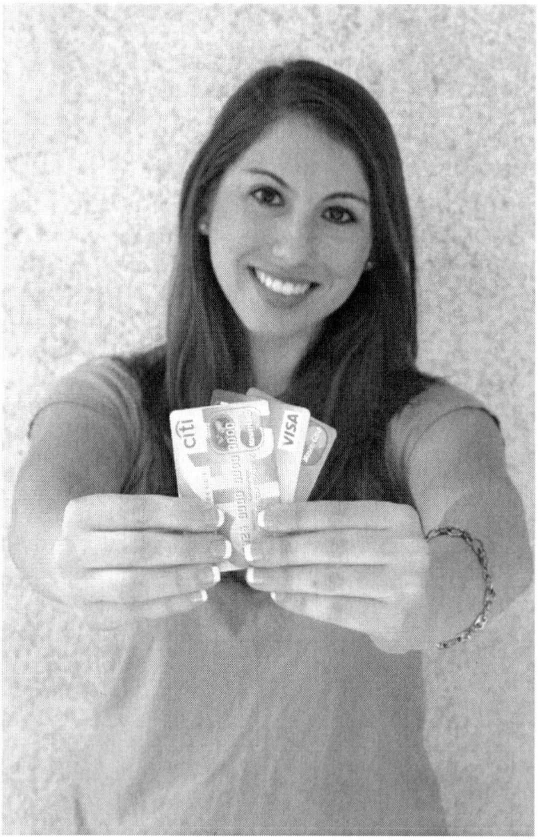
citi
VISA

How Your Credit Can Impact Your Job Search

Imagine that you applied for your dream job. Now picture that you got through the interview process with flying colors and the employer says it's between you and one other candidate, all we have to do is run our back ground check and a credit report. How do you feel now? Are you still confident you got the job? This is a true life lesson for many Americans. If you have not shown that you are a responsible adult who pays their obligations on time, what does that tell a prospective employer? What if the other candidate has good credit with scores over 700? What if a security clearance is a condition of the job?

Okay, maybe you are the candidate with good credit scores. Is it high enough to impress this potential employer? Does the other candidate have higher scores?

Regardless of which one of these candidates you are, know that the next time you apply for a job or even a higher position within your current company, your credit report holds weight in their decision. Not all employers run a credit report for employment, but the numbers are high and continue to increase. You need to take your credit seriously.

(IMAGE CREDIT TO MILES STUART AT FREEDIGITALPHOTOS.NET)

Real Life Scenario - Co-Signing Lesson

One of my clients learned that their credit score had decreased substantially and was denied for a refinance on her personal residence. She had no idea why the decrease in score. She was paying her bills on time. Her husband's credit was not affected, but without her income they couldn't qualify for the lower interest rate. They asked for my assistance. When we reviewed their credit report we learned that an auto loan, that she was a co-signer on for her son, has not been paid in months. It was in default. My client told me that she was told that she wouldn't be obligated to make the payments and that they just needed my income for my son to qualify. We immediately called her son, who told his mother, "don't worry, I'm taking care of it." I explained to the son that he has damaged his mother's credit and that if he didn't resolve the back payments immediately that the creditor has the right to reposes the automobile. This was a rude awakening for both the mother and her son. The mother had co-signed for the auto without the husband's knowledge. Needless to say this caused some issues. The son didn't have the funds, so the parents paid the back payments. Needless to say, the parents were not happy about the situation. After that, they made the son make the payments to them prior to the due date and the parents made sure that the payments were made on time from there forward. However, the damage was done. It will take quite some time to pass before the mother's credit score will regain those lost points. The bigger picture is the refinance that they were denied for. They were going to save $350 a month, on a 30 year mortgage. This co-signing education cost them approximately $126,000 ($350/mo. X 12 months a year X 30 years = $126,000). That became a very expensive lesson.

Let's "Soar." Life Is Better With Good Credit

For over 25 years I have been a Consumer Advocate. I have been advising those who yearn for answers on how to better their financial life and help people increase their credit ratings. I have taken consumers step-by-step through the process of identifying errors on their reports, disputing inaccurate information and increasing their potential scores in the process. One-by-one, they tell me how much better their lives are with good credit. They have taken control of their finances and are provided new opportunities. Instead of paying high interested rates and annual fees, they are being offered low rates and either pay no annual fees or they get them waived. I am proud to share the secrets of how to do it yourself. It is rewarding. The information in this book can benefit everyone. Every item on a credit report is valuable when determining your credit score. Your credit report is changing every day. As the components of your report change, thus the score is evolving too.

When it comes down to the basics, remember to make your payments on time, EVERY TIME and stay within budget. Keep your utilization ratios low (do not use more than sixty percent of your credit limit) and do not close paid accounts in good standing. I hope that you will setup a plan of action and get your free credit reports. Do not hesitate to work with data furnishers and the credit bureaus to remove erroneous, out of date, and unverifiable information from your report. Take the steps necessary my friend, to make your credit score SOAR.

Credit Terminology and Acronyms

AG: Attorney General
ARM: Adjustable Rate Mortgage
AR: Account Review (soft pulls by creditors)
AU: Authorized User
BBB: Better Business Bureau
BK: Bankruptcy
BK13: Chapter 13 Bankruptcy
BK7: Chapter 7 Bankruptcy
C&D: Cease and Desist (stop collections)
CA: Collection Agency
CAP 1: Capital One
CB: Credit Bureau
CBR: Credit Bureau Report
CC: Credit Card
CCC: Credit Card Company
CCCS: Consumer Credit Counseling Services
CE Score: Credit Expert Score
CK: Credit Keeper
CL: Credit Limit
CM: Certified Mail
CMRRR: Certified Mail Return Receipt Requested
CO: Charge off OR Collections
CR: Credit Report
CRA: Credit Reporting Agency

CRO: Credit Repair Organization
CRRR: Certified mail, Return Receipt Requested
CU: Credit Union
CW: Credit Watch
DC: Debt Collector
DDA: Direct Deposit Account
DEROG: Derogatory trade line, an item on your credit file that is negative in any way.
DF: Data Furnisher (also FOI)
DMP: Debt Management Plan
DOI: Department of Insurance
DOFD: Date of First Delinquency
DOLA: Date of Last Activity
DTI: Debt to Income
DV: Debt Validation
EFT: Electronic Funds Transfer
E-Oscar: Electronic program data furnishers use to communicate with CRA's
EQ: Equifax
EQ CWG: Equifax Credit Watch Gold
ETA: Edited to Add
EX: Experian
Experica: Similar to FICO, as reported by Trans Union.

FACTA: Fair and Accurate Credit Transaction Act. Revisions to FCRA
Fair Isaac: Similar to FICO, as reported by Experian.
FAKO: Fake credit score, i.e., any other than the FICO
FCBA: Fair Credit Billing Act
FCRA: Fair Credit Reporting Act
FCRA Compliance Date: Often called "DOFD", the date the

reporting SOL is based off of
FDCPA: Fair Debt Collection Practices Act
FHA: Federal Housing Administration
FICO: Fair Isaac Company, the company that created the mathematical formula used to score credit worthiness of consumers
FICO: Fair Isaac score
FIFO: First In, First Out. Usually refers to how your letters are answered.
FOI: Furnisher of Information
Freddie Mac: Federal Home Loan Mortgage Corporation (FHLM)
FRCP: Federal Rules of Civil Procedure
FTC: Federal Trade Commission.
Goodwill adjustment: Adjustment made to your credit report in response to your Goodwill letter.
GW: Goodwill letter
HELOC: Home Equity Line of Credit
HIPAA: Health Insurance Portability & Accountability Act of 1996,Public Law 104-191
IIB: Included In Bankruptcy
INQ: Inquiry
ITS: Intent To Sue
L/N: Lexis/Nexis (Another sneaky CRA-type)
LOC: Line of credit
MCK: My Credit Keeper
OC: Original creditor
OP: Original Post or Poster
PFD: Pay for Deletion
PIF: Paid In Full
PMI: Private Mortgage Insurance

PP: Permissible Purpose (to pull your credit report)
RR: Return Receipt
RRR: Return Receipt Requested
SASE: Self-Addressed Stamped Envelope
SIF: Settled In Full
SOL: Statute of limitations
TILA: Truth in Lending Act
TL: Trade line
TU: TransUnion
UCC: Uniformed Commercial Code
UDF: Universal Data Form

Consumer Resources

AmeriSell, Inc. - AmeriSell Credit Consulting
www.amerisell.com

amerisell@live.com

Federal Trade Commission (FTC) www.consumer.ftc.gov

Free Credit Report www.annualcreditreport.com or call 1-877-322-8228

Experian www.experian.com

P.O. Box 2002, Allen, TX 75013 (888) 397-3742 or (800) 397-3742

TransUnion www.transunion.com

2 Baldwin Place, P.O. Box 1000, Chester, PA 19022 (800) 888-4213 or (800) 680-7289

Equifax www.equifax.com

P.O. Box 740241, Atlanta, GA 30374
 (800) 685-1111 or (800) 525-6285

How to File a Complaint go
to www.consumer.ftc.gov/media

Mortgage Help/Consumer Financial Protection
Bureau consumerfinance.gov/mortgagehelp

Fair Debt Collection Practices Act (FDCPA)
www.consumer.ftc.gov

The FTC enforces the FDCPA to protect consumers from deceptive, abusive, or unfair tactics

Disclaimer:

This book is sold with the understanding that neither the author is engaged in rendering legal, accounting, or other professional services or advice by releasing this book. Each individual situation is unique. Therefore, if legal or financial advice or other expert assistance is required in a specific situation, the services of a competent professional should be sought to ensure that the situation has been evaluated carefully and appropriately. The author disclaims any liability, loss, or risk resulting directly or indirectly, from the use or application of any contents of this book.

Copyright 2014 © All rights reserved

Printed in Canada